LANVIN

Translated from the French by Harriet Mason

First published in Great Britain in 1997
by Thames and Hudson Ltd, London

Copyright © 1997 Éditions Assouline, Paris

British Library Cataloguing-in-Publication Data
A catalogue record for this book is available from
the British Library

ISBN 0-500-01816-2

Printed and bound in Italy

LANVIN

Text by Élisabeth Barillé

Thames and Hudson

everything is there, classified, filed and collected in dark bindings that are indistinguishable from account books except for the fact that the year's date is stamped on the spines in fine gold – the scallops of mother of pearl and mica, the Greek key pattern borders of coral, the sprinklings of pearls and interlaced silver threads.

Everything is there, every kind of ornamental knot, every silk trimming, every hat design, and innumerable sketches where a vermilion highlight on a belt, a wash of orange on a sleeveless bodice, or the dark shimmer of a sable stole all look as if they have been applied just a moment ago.

The Lanvin archives are fascinating for two reasons. They have, firstly, a unique importance in the history of fashion. They include samples of beadwork and embroidery covering nearly twenty-five years, the complete set of drawings for the couture collections, more than five hundred designs ranging from wedding dresses to theatre costumes, as well as a mass of other documents assembled by Jeanne Lanvin herself. This hoard is carefully preserved at 22 Rue du Faubourg Saint-Honoré, the head office of the couture house. Secondly, the archive is particularly remarkable today for its vitality, which seems to stem from more than just the indulgent mood of a period when time stood still for a while, apparently on a whim. The striking array of colours is reminiscent in its variety of the poet Ronsard, or a dream-like rose garden; it is impossible to overlook the clear but discreet signals of an unspoken creed.

●

Jeanne Lanvin was a woman of few words. In the world of rustling silks and gossip into which she was drawn as she went from client to client, this is a disconcerting characteristic. Although she was unconventional, like Paul Poiret, and imperious, like Gabrielle Chanel, she chose to stay in the background. Silent and reserved, almost taciturn, invariably wearing her trademark black suit with minimal white details, she seemed to distance herself from her society clients. They were not amused when told: 'We have instructions not to disturb her, she doesn't particularly want to speak to you.'

What was it that preoccupied her? Some claimed it was hopes for her daughter Marguerite's success; others were sure she thought only about the success of her collections, which could be said to be the same thing. Marguerite was a pink and white Lanvin beauty from head to toe, and the couturier's only child. A brilliant marriage gave her a title and a new first name: Marie-Blanche, Comtesse de Polignac. Her elegance caused a sensation in the salons; her pure voice was perfect for performing Poulenc songs at the Sunday musical gatherings patronized by the cream of Paris society. Lanvin's daughter more than fulfilled the extraordinarily modest fashion designer's private dreams. The focus of her admiration, she was also her muse; she lived and worked for her alone. Louise de Vilmorin, an authority on society psychology, declared: 'She dazzled everyone with her work, but she did it for the sake of dazzling her daughter.'

For Lanvin, more than for any other designer of haute couture, fashion and love were indistinguishable because they had the same starting point: Marguerite-Marie-Blanche. As a child she was dressed in fairy-like clothes; as an adolescent she was adorned like a woman. Later she was presented as a young woman who was still partly a child, in dresses with a renewed vitality and naturalness. Jeanne Lanvin came to mean eternal youth; in this way she was able to relive her own youth, which she had sacrificed to her work.

Lanvin was thirteen when she began to earn her living. There was nothing unusual in this; in Paris there were hundreds of dressmakers' errand girls who, like her, did the rounds of clients with armfuls of their orders – dresses, hats or trimmings. But there were few with her determination. She was nicknamed 'The Little Omnibus', because she ran along behind the horse-drawn bus to save herself the fare. Five years later, at the age of eighteen, when she finished her apprenticeship as a milliner with 'Madame Felix' at 15 Rue du Faubourg Saint-Honoré, she set up in business on her own. Her workroom in an attic in Rue du Marché Saint-Honoré was a modest beginning, but she was undaunted. She had boundless energy, capital of one gold *louis*, one client to back her, and credit of three hundred francs with her suppliers.

those who had faith in her were proved right. She moved twice, to larger and better located premises, in less time than it took to construct the Arcimboldesque concoctions of flowers, fruit and feathers that were the crowning glory of the feminine form at the turn of the century. Hats with the Lanvin label had not yet achieved the understated luxury for which they would be famous from 1910 onwards. Her first move was to the Rue Saint-Honoré, her second to the Rue des Mathurins. Like her contemporary, the writer Paul Morand, Jeanne Lanvin was a young woman in a hurry, and this meant constantly creating new designs and showing what she was capable of. Those who have never felt a sense of vocation might call her ambitious, but a better word would be single-minded. She was utterly committed to her talent, her passion for her work, the pride she felt in providing for her whole family (her brothers very soon joined her in her workrooms), and to the middle-class belief in the virtue of work.

So what did she think of the leisured class – the courtesans, society ladies and unconventional beauties who commissioned her to adorn their carefree heads? She looked on them with detachment rather than envy, from the standpoint of a woman who was secure in a role that she had created for herself and which she would not change for anything. She got into the habit of presenting rather an austere appearance, with a somewhat straitlaced quality that almost made her more conspicious than she would have been if she had dressed extravagantly. Nevertheless, Lanvin captivated the Italian aristocrat Emilio di Pietro when they met at the Longchamp racecourse, that open-air theatre of social life where she made a study of style and bearing.

They were married in 1895 and divorced in 1903. Their meteoric union produced a star, their daughter Marguerite, born in 1897. In the excitement of new motherhood, the businesswoman suddenly saw the possibility of a new project: children's clothes. She started to sew especially for 'Ririte', as she called her, decorating an organza christening robe with a deftly worked scattering of bright yellow daisies. Gradually she designed an entire wardrobe, the most dazzling ever worn by a child, sewn with love and inspiration. There was a dark blazer with gold buttons, an ermine coat fringed with black, sleeveless dresses shirred around the hem, gaiters of *peau d'ange* or angel skin, embroidered gloves and a Neapolitan cap made of silver mesh. Everything was light, subtle and simple: Jeanne Lanvin had just invented children's fashion. The clothes had quite a different emphasis from the concentration in adult clothing on sophistication and appearances;

they were miracles of hand-sewing, created with good taste, but allowing childhood room to breathe.

Encouraged by the number of orders from her clients for clothes for their own daughters, Lanvin opened a children's department. It was to be the turning point of her career. The charm of the clothes added a defining characteristic to all her work. The quality of workmanship, the attention given to the choice of colours and fabrics, were the features which, little by little, as if spontaneously, became established as the essence of Lanvin. Something which she had originally conceived for little girls on an impulse, unwittingly, at a time when her maternal infatuation was overruling her business sense, would suddenly become all the rage among Parisiennes.

When Lanvin joined the Syndicat de la Couture in 1909, her girls' and ladies' departments had already made an unprecedented impact on the success of her house, which was hardly affected by the Great War.

In 1918 she took over the whole building at 22 Rue du Faubourg Saint-Honoré. It included two workrooms for semi-tailored clothes, two for tailored ones, one for lingerie, one for hats, one that was used as a design studio, and two that were given over to embroidery; the latter was a speciality which Lanvin, unlike other couturiers, did not entrust to outside workers. During the 1920s, when her evening dresses reached a matchless brilliance, their immaculate beadwork was established as one of her firm's signatures. In 1925, the Lanvin ateliers employed more than eight hundred people, not including the sales assistants. At every collection three hundred outfits were shown from which her clients would choose around thirty. Among these clients were many American women, who thought nothing of making a special trip across the Atlantic. Lanvin had already been in 1915 to San Francisco, where she would have responded eagerly to the vigour of the New World and the studied casualness described in his novels by Scott Fitzgerald, inspired by the delicate features of his wife, the unpredictable Zelda. In 1925 she launched her first great perfume, which was very successful in the United States.

bit by bit an empire was established, one which continued to bear the personal hallmark of Jeanne Lanvin. It now included sports clothes, furs, men's fashions and even interior decoration. Here Lanvin was keen to add her personal touch too, anticipating by several decades the importance attached by modern designers to their 'house style'. With this in mind she oversaw the opening of a shop at 15 Rue du Faubourg Saint-Honoré, which, in keeping with the character of the proprietress, was expected to be decorated in a discreet and sober style.

It is hard to imagine the Parisians' amazement when they first saw the sumptuous and fantastic decor. The huge doors were covered with spectacular bronze reliefs, the oak woodwork displayed sensuous carvings of human and animal forms, the lift-cage was of gilded latticework. All this was the work of Armand-Albert Rateau, a decorator to whom Lanvin had been introduced by the couturier Paul Poiret. Then aged thirty-eight, he was the son of a Burgundian bootmaker, and had entered the Ecole Boule at the age of twelve. He won the admiration of the couturier, who immediately commissioned him to decorate the interior of her mansion in the Rue Barbet-de-Jouy, and later of her villas at Cannes and Le Touquet. Following Lanvin Décoration, their collaboration continued at the Théâtre Daunou, as well as at other branches of her shops, until 1927, when she launched 'Arpège'. Lanvin dedicated the perfume to her daughter, and asked Rateau to design the sophisticated black ball-shaped bottle to contain it. The sensual and mysterious fragrance was created by the perfumer André Fraysse, using Bulgarian roses, jasmine from Grasse, honeysuckle and lily of the valley. Some of the drawings in the archive suggest that Rateau may also have worked on the design for the bottle's gold label. This shows the couturier and her daughter getting ready for a fancy-dress ball, and is usually attributed to Paul Iribe. It is still the trademark of the house, and 'Arpège' remains one of the best known features of the Lanvin empire.

The collaboration between Lanvin and Rateau was full of contrasts. There was the youthful spirit of her style, fresh as peonies, and the exuberant world of the eclectic aesthete Rateau, who created unexpected juxtapositions of form and ornament from his fascination with Babylon, Knossos and Pompeii. However, there were profound affinities between them as well as what Baudelaire described as 'discordant words . . . which mingle in the distance'; their approaches were distinct but complementary. It shows in their shared love of materials, the classical harmony of the lines and the meticulously planned attention to detail. For example, an evening dress with a patiently worked galaxy of pearls and mother-of-pearl; pieces of occasional furniture finely carved with bees, lizards and daisies; a formal coat with trailing sleeves covered in gold lace and sable; a chaise-longue supported by four bronze does; a dressing table designed for the mansion in the Rue Barbet-de-Jouy consisting of a double mirror decorated with daisies and butterflies, standing on four narrow bronze legs surmounted by lotus flowers and wreathed with daisies. Lanvin–Rateau meant a shared ideal of refinement, and a unique flair for drawing on the intimate stuff of dreams to fashion a reality of their own. They had a shared vision but did they also have a shared style?

althewordugh the use of the word style is almost unavoidable, Lanvin played it down in a deliberately provocative article in *Vogue* in 1945. It is an important document as it remains one of the couturier's rare personal statements. 'For many years now, those who have seen my collections have always been eager to define a Lanvin style. I know it is often discussed, nevertheless I have never limited myself to a particular kind of clothing, and have never sought to emphasize a specific style. On the contrary, I make great efforts every season to capture a certain mood, and use my own interpretation of events around me to put my fleeting concept into tangible form.' Though understated, this is a startlingly modern declaration. Lanvin was defending nothing less than the right of the designer to do unexpected things, as well as more predictable ones, to be consistent or impulsive, lighthearted or serious – in short, to be herself. Away with creeds! Lanvin made no claims for anything other than her wish to 'contribute to the spell of femininity'.

She was championing freedom, informality, love of the moment, as if time were unimportant. Certainly one of the characteristics of a Lanvin outfit was the wish to blur the usual distinctions between women and young girls, with a fluid silhouette, flattering to a growing shape as well as one approaching middle age. And there is no doubt that the time was ripe for behind-the-scenes revolutions such as this. The Olympian Duchesse de Guermantes, in Proust's novel *Remembrance of Things Past*, restricted by her corset as much as by convention, no longer dictated current taste. It was Irène, the ambitious heroine of Paul Morand's 1924 novel, *Lewis et Irène*, who compelled the world to acknowledge her thirst for life, to be a businesswoman in the morning, traveller in the afternoon and lover at night.

For her and all who wanted to emulate her, Jeanne Lanvin produced between 1920 and 1935 a classic dress suited to varieties of mood and build, with slit sides, a loose top, and either sleeved or sleeveless. Also specifically designed for the changing moods of the young shingle-haired pioneers was a black taffetta dress with either short sleeves and a few flowers on the bodice, or long sleeves and a deep décolleté embellished with paste ornaments.

One of the couturier's concerns was never to be dictated to by the preoccupations of the period in which she lived. In 1925 the spare styling of Art Deco made a widespread impact; but though its austere lacquer and chrome provided the ideal setting for Gabrielle Chanel to develop her own language to maximum effect, Lanvin had no hesitation in making stylish clothes that were delightfully dated. They were close fitting, with the high waists of the Second Empire; or they had long sleeves and shawl collars, with distinct echoes of the fifteenth-century *Lady with Unicorn* tapestry. Or they had flounced skirts, cartridge pleats, and décolletés with netting inserts based on old fashion plates. Debutantes chose to make their first appearance in society in some of her elegant and simple outfits.

'Modern clothes need a certain romantic feel,' she declared, emphasizing that couturiers 'should take care not to become too everyday and practical'. The many wedding dresses she designed were clearly created in this spirit. Jeanne Lanvin, perhaps in common with all women, had a deep attachment to the romantic, one which was hardly affected by the fashion of the day.

It is not surprising, therefore, that her designs attracted actresses and women writers, such as the poet Anna de Noailles, the novelist Louise de Vilmorin, the American star of silent films Mary Pickford, the actress Cécile Sorel, and of course Yvonne Printemps, for whom she made stage clothes as well as everyday outfits. These were clothes to act in rather than theatrical costumes; the difference was in the cut. Actresses know how to make an impression, and they rightly responded to the radical character of clothes which allowed for freedom of movement. For her part Jeanne Lanvin was in her element. In 1923 alone she designed the costumes for no fewer than seventeen shows. She constructed a full-sized stage set in her atelier specially for the fittings. Among her successes were the ethereal tunics she designed for *Amphytrion 38*, the play by Jean Giraudoux, and the wonderful white silk dress famously worn by Arletty as Garance in the film *Les Enfants du Paradis*. 'When you are constantly thinking about new designs', said Lanvin, 'everything you see is transformed and adapted to whatever is in hand. The process happens naturally and becomes an instinct, a truth, a necessity, another language.'

as we already know, 'Madame', as the plaque on her office door called her, said little. But, for all that, everything she did spoke for her. However much she tried to deny it, she did in fact create a style. An unbroken sequence of harmonious echoes links each design to the following one, from one decade to the next, finely wrought, polished, picked up again and again, whether in the most delicate clothes or in the grandest, always with concern for detail pushed to its limit. This clearly had its roots in her apprentice years, when, as a form of relaxation as well as a means of earning some pocket money, Lanvin made dolls' clothes. Her children's clothes and lingerie, two of the most successful aspects of her business, were based on the high precision skills learned at that time.

For her there was no revolutionary look, just her work as a couturier and an unquenchable thirst for seeing, learning and collecting for which she had an unlimited and dazzling capacity.

lanvin's office was more of a connoisseur's study than a dress designer's studio, full of thousands of treasures gleaned from around the world by someone with a sensitive, resourceful and enquiring mind. There were sculptures, books, jewels, as well as an astonishing collection of fabrics and clothes; among them Indian saris, Persian silks, mandarins' robes, Breton waistcoats, embroidered African tunics and Coptic embroideries. It was a priceless booty, meticulously labelled and catalogued with a bibliophile's obsessive care; Lanvin even called it her fabric library. By giving it an air of mystery, she gave it a life of its own. She was like a bee, tasting everything in order to make her exceptionally delicious honey. It might be a Mantegna virgin, a Byzantine mosaic, the statues of Saint Mark's in Venice, or a particular spot of red on a Holbein painting. Her art blossomed with every discovery. As for the lavender blue that is nowadays called Lanvin blue, she saw it first in a fresco by Fra Angelico; giving herself a stiff neck, she said later, from peering at it for so long.

The Lanvin colours were exclusive to her. As well as Lanvin blue there was a coral, pale pink, cerise, mauve and almond green. Lanvin undoubtedly developed her innate sense of colour through her contact with painters, both those she knew, for instance the Nabi painter Edouard Vuillard, and those whose work she collected, such as Auguste Rodin and the enigmatic Odilon Redon. She created masterly harmonies for her clothes, using a delicate palette of graded colours or soft monochromes. Her perfectionist standards led her to build a dyeing works in 1923, and from then on her house colours were not only subtle but inimitable. Sometimes she teamed them with silver, and continued to use her favourite black; combining it with white, she created the amazing graphic motifs which made her dresses and suits so distinctive.

Other strong points were embroidery and beading. She used pearls and sequins, of course, but also tiny pieces of mica, coral, minute shells, gold and silver threads, ribbons and raffia. The variety of materials was matched by the variety of motifs. The influences were very mixed; she was sometimes inspired by Coptic and Celtic crosses, and firework bursts, and there were even hints of Zen. It is impossible to give a comprehensive idea of these geometric cantatas, other than to underline recurring themes, the leitmotifs of what could be called a silent art of the fugue.

The daisy represented Jeanne's inexpressible passion for her daughter. There was the heart shape too. Often stylized, sometimes indecipherable at first glance, it was the basis for many of the embroidery and beadwork designs. Another consistent motif was the knot, and certain leaf shapes, such as sweet bay, ivy and olive – trees of infinite symbolism. The stylized Art Deco rose, a favourite of Paul Poiret, was also used, sometimes embroidered or beaded, or sewn on petal by petal to give an effect of lightness and movement. Her use of beadwork and embroidery reached its peak between 1920 and 1925, and was slowly replaced by attention to the fabrics themselves.

Lamé was first used in the Lanvin collections in 1930; by 1936 and the daring creation of a silver lamé wedding dress for the Princess of Alcántara, there was a new emphasis on so-called atelier work. There were satins bisected by parallel lines of stitching, or with smocked plastron bodices and shoulder wings; coiled braid work, narrow cording to accentuate the structure of the tailored clothes; ruching with pinked edges; intricate folds producing astonishing optical effects; appliqué, flounces and tucks. It all added up to a range of effects which showed an intimate knowledge of fabrics. As she said herself: 'A design inevitably reflects the artistic motifs stored in one's memory, drawing on those which are the most alive, new and fertile all at the same time'. Jeanne Lanvin continued to vary these endlessly right up to the 1940s.

every designer has a secret. The discreet Jeanne Lanvin always took good care not to unveil a mystery which perhaps unintentionally she continued to deepen. During the fifty years following her death, a succession of gifted designers have served at the head of her house, but the imprint of Jeanne Lanvin herself is as rich and enigmatic as ever.

There are several images of her to choose from. There is the devoted mother. There is the impassioned but modest pioneer, as committed to her work as she was at the beginning of her career. There is the traveller, constantly on the lookout for new visual stimuli. There is the aesthete, who in the heart of Paris at 16 Rue Barbet-de-Jouy realized her dreams in a luxurious Eastern decor, with marble statues here and there, chased bronze Arab decorations, pale ivory coloured columns, and wall hangings of Lanvin blue picked out in silver. Or there is simply the incomparable dress designer, whose invaluable lessons about freedom and a fresh approach have clearly struck a chord with the designers of today.

RÊVERIE

ROBES, DE JEANNE LANVIN

Nuit Etoilée

Nuit Etoilée.

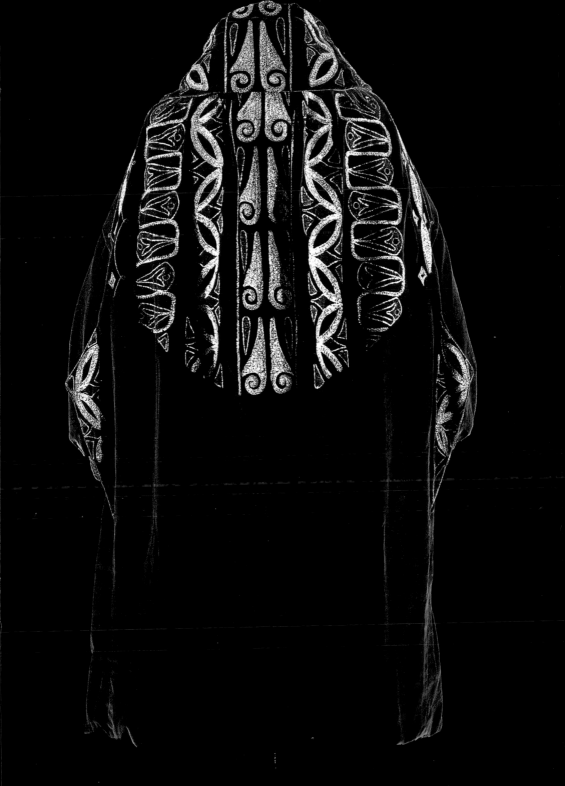

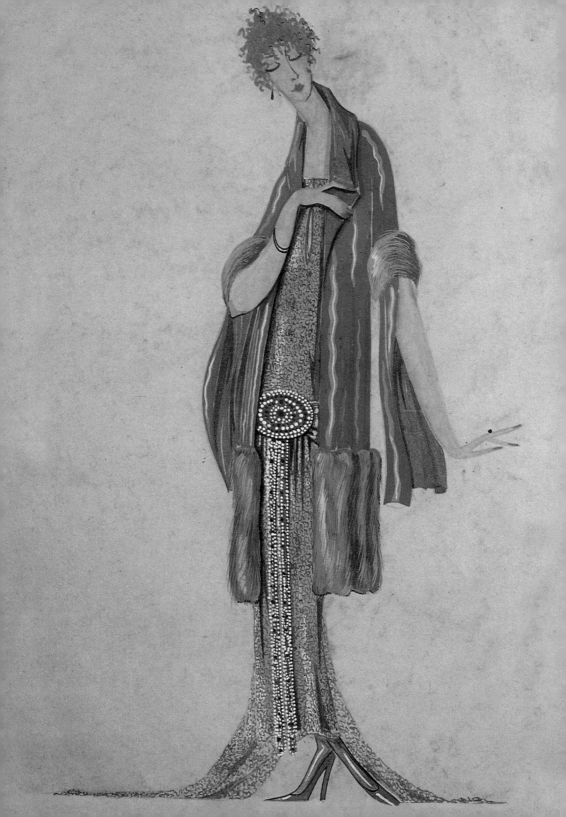

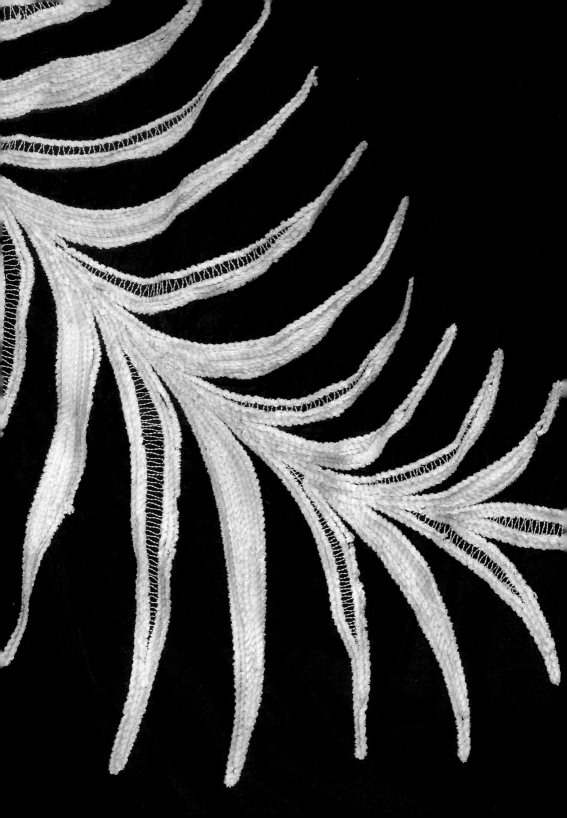

Mlle CÉCILE SOREL.

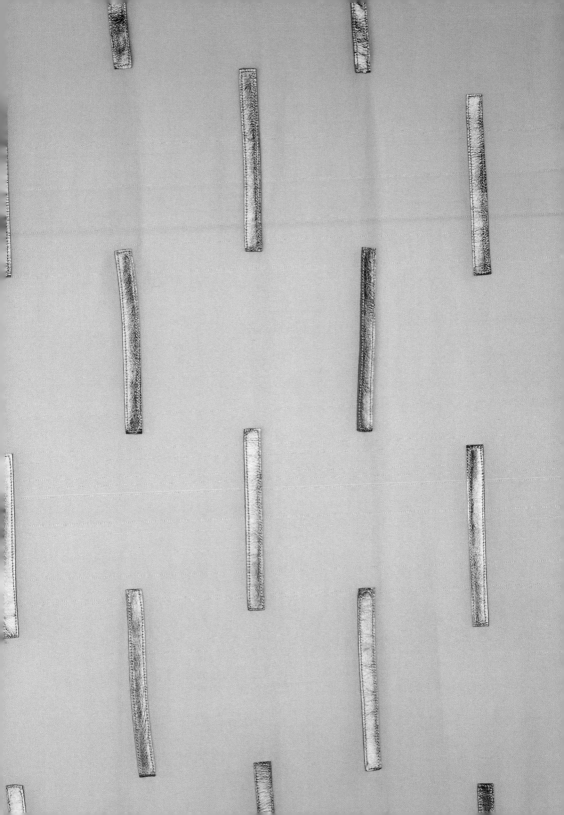

LES ALLÉES

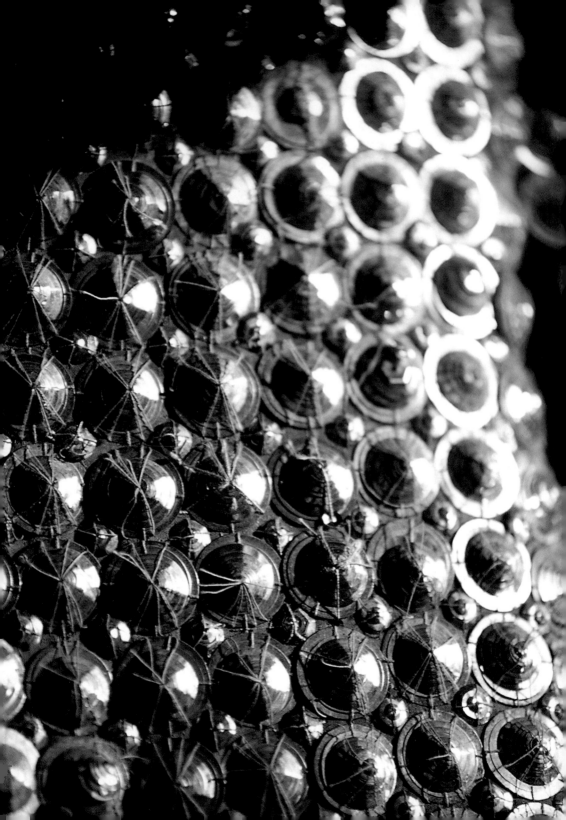

Chronology

1867 Birth of Jeanne Lanvin 1 January at 35 Rue Mazarine, Paris. Her father, Constantin Bernard Lanvin, was a journalist; the family consisted of nine boys and a girl.

1883 Begins work trimming hats in Madame Felix's workshop at 15 Rue du Faubourg Saint-Honoré.

1885 Sets up her own workshop in Rue du Marché Saint-Honoré, with the financial and moral support of her first client.

1889 Starts her own millinery business at 16 Rue Boissy-d'Anglas.

1895 Marries the Italian aristocrat Emilio di Pietro. Their marriage is brief and ends in divorce in 1903.

1897 Birth of Marguerite. Jeanne Lanvin makes an entire wardrobe for her daughter.

1901 Jeanne Lanvin's name is included in the fashion yearbook. Her premises now occupy 16–20 Rue Boissy-d'Anglas. She designs, for Edmond Rostand, the first of many ceremonial robes for members of the Académie Française.

1907 Marries the journalist Xavier Melet, who later becomes the French consul in Manchester, England.

1908 Opens her children's clothes department.

1909 With the opening of her new ladies' and girls' departments she becomes a fully-fledged couturier, and joins the Syndicat de la Couture.

1915 Exhibits at the San Francisco World Fair.

1920 The interior decorator Armand-Albert Rateau (1882–1938), then aged 38, becomes a close friend; he designs the interior of her new shop, Lanvin Décoration, at 15 Rue du Faubourg Saint-Honoré, as well as that of her later shop at 22 Rue du Faubourg Saint-Honore. He also decorates Lanvin's mansion at Rue Barbet-de-Jouy in Paris's 7th *arrondissement*, the Théâtre Daunou, branches of her shops and her other homes.

1923 A dyeing factory is built at Nanterre to produce the subtle colours of the 'Lanvin palette'. Later the Lanvin Parfum laboratories are established there for André Fraysse.

1925 Jeanne Lanvin acts as vice-president of the Pavillon de l'Elégance at the Exposition Internationale des Arts Décoratifs, Paris. Her couture house now has 23 ateliers, employing up to 800 people, excluding the sales assistants. Three hundred outfits are shown in every collection. Lanvin branches are opened in Cannes and Le Touquet. Her first perfume, 'My Sin', is launched; its heady mixture of heliotrope and tuberoses is an immediate success in the United States. Marguerite marries the comte Jean de Polignac and changes her name to Marie-Blanche. It is the beginning of a high society life which greatly benefits the couture house.

A design with an oriental flavour, using embroidered and laméed lace, with beads and paste decoration. Worn by Yvonne Printemps in L'Amour masqué at the Théâtre Edouard VII in 1924. Gouache © Lanvin Estate.

1926 On 9 January Jeanne Lanvin is created Chevalier de la Légion d'Honneur. Her nephew Maurice Lanvin becomes the director of a new men's department at 15 Rue du Faubourg Saint-Honoré; she also opens new departments for furs and lingerie.

1927 The perfume 'Arpège' is launched, contained in a magnificent round black bottle with a gold stopper, designed by Armand-Albert Rateau. It is decorated with a golden vignette, which becomes her trademark, showing Jeanne Lanvin holding out her hands to her daughter. The fragrance is created by the 25-year-old perfumer, André Fraysse. Novelist Louise de Vilmorin describes it as 'combining the smell of flowers, fruit, furs and leaves'. This masterpiece is still regarded as the essence of the world of Lanvin. New shops are opened at Deauville, Biarritz, Barcelona and Buenos Aires.

1933 The perfume 'Scandal' is launched, an aura of ambergris with a hint of leather; also 'Eau de Lanvin'.

1934 Launch of the eau-de-cologne 'Rumeur'.

1935 Lanvin outfits are modelled at a gala held on board the *Normandie*, on its maiden voyage to New York. Jeanne Lanvin takes part in the International Exhibition in Brussels.

1937 Takes part in the Exposition Universelle, Paris.

1938 Jeanne Lanvin is created Officier de la Légion d'Honneur; the eulogy is delivered by Sacha Guitry.

1939 Takes part in the Golden Gate International Exposition, San Francisco, and the World Fair in New York.

1945 Takes part in the exhibition 'Théâtre de la mode' (an international relaunch of haute couture after the war).

1946 Jeanne Lanvin dies on 6 July, aged 79. Her daughter Marie-Blanche becomes chairman and managing director of Jeanne Lanvin and Lanvin Parfums.

1950 Marie-Blanche hands over the haute-couture side to the Spanish designer Antonio Canovas del Castillo.

1963 The Belgian Jules-François Crahay takes over from Castillo. He is awarded three *Dés d'Or* ('Golden Thimbles'), in recognition of his work.

1985 The haute couture is handed over to Maryll Lanvin.

1990 Claude Montana is appointed and presents five haute-couture collections. He is later awarded two *Dés d'Or*.

1993 The House of Lanvin withdraws from haute couture and concentrates on luxury ladies' ready-to-wear clothes and accessories, while continuing the men's lines and made-to-measure sportswear.

Design by Ocimar Versolato for the Autumn/Winter 1996–97 Lanvin collection; a long dress in black satin silk. Photo by Jean-Loup Sieff. © Lanvin Estate.

Lanvin

Spherical bottle: 'Arpège' owed its success in 1927 as much to its wonderful bottle as to André Fraysse's sensual fragrance. The black ball devised by Armand-Albert Rateau was made in several limited and numbered editions, including this version in amaranth-coloured porcelain made by the Manufacture Nationale de Sèvres. © Lanvin Estate. **Jeanne Lanvin and her daughter dressed for a ball.** This photograph, taken in 1907, inspired the drawing by Paul Iribe which became the Lanvin trademark. © Lanvin Estate.

'Rêverie': Drawn about 1924 by the artist Georges Lepape for the *Gazette du bon ton,* these two children's dresses illustrate the youthful bias of the Lanvin style. Lanvin Estate. © 1997 ADAGP. Women who wanted a youthful look were drawn to Lanvin; this **dress of black and cream taffeta and tulle,** decorated with flowers made of velvet ribbon, has a typically demure décolleté. It was named 'Balsamine', and dates from 1924; a similar model is owned by the Lanvin Estate. © The Metropolitan Museum of Art.

This **short evening cape** is richly decorated with motifs in pink beadwork and silver thread, with a contrasting fur edging. It has a matching mesh cap, beaded and embroidered. It was designed in 1926, the same year that Jeanne Lanvin was created Chevalier de la Légion d'Honneur. Gouache. © Lanvin Estate. **Robe de style,** summer 1924: black silk taffeta with green silk and sequin-embroidered medallions and silver corded net. Gift of Mrs Albert Spalding, 1962. © The Metropolitan Museum of Art.

A dressed doll: From when she was very young, Jeanne Lanvin had a weakness for dressing dolls. The best known are the delicate figures with plaster limbs and heads that were displayed in her shop windows, dressed in miniature versions of her current designs. Jeanne Lanvin also dressed Duret's wax dolls, and dolls belonging to her most faithful clients' children; some of these small marvels are now owned by the Lanvin Estate. © Laziz Hamani. **The design for the dress worn by the doll** in the shop window. This is made of black taffeta with tulle sleeves, and embroidered with mirror sequins and glass beads. It was called 'Nuit etoilée' ('starry night'). Gouache. © Lanvin Estate.

A dress of pink and grey shot taffeta called 'Vénitienne' ('Venetian'), on account of the style of the decoration, made with green and copper-coloured beads. The same design was made for a shop window doll. Lanvin Estate. © Photo Laziz Hamani.
An example of **embroidery and beading** from the 1920s. The arabesques made with beads and tinted shells illustrate Jeanne Lanvin's use of a variety of materials to decorate her clothes. Lanvin Estate. © Photo Laziz Hamani.

Placed like an exotic butterfly on the black taffeta, **a huge bow** made of beads, paste and silver embroidery contrasts effectively with the simplicity of this design shown at the 1925 Exposition International des Arts Décoratifs. © Collection Viollet. Among the many embroidered motifs, **the bow** was one of the most frequently used. Made of beads, paste or pieces of mica and coral, it was often used to emphasize the waistline. © Photo Sarah Moon.

Examples of the great variety of materials used in the **embroidered decorations**; beads, glass, metal, silk thread, and more unusual elements such as shells. Lanvin Estate. © Photo Laziz Hamani.

Jupiter: Presented in the winter of 1919, this evening coat of purple velvet lined with marigold-coloured satin makes a feature of the pure lines of the Art Deco style. The gold lamé details accentuate the depth of the colour. Lanvin Estate. © Photo Laziz Hamani.

Jeanne Lanvin in her office, choosing some embroideries; photographed by Roger Schall in 1936. She is wearing one of the black and white suits she was particularly fond of and a necklace of large pearls, her favourite jewels. © Photo Roger Schall.

A dress of black organdie with beige organdie borders, decorated with white beads. It was made in 1924 for Jeanne Lanvin's friend Yvonne Printemps. Gouache and dress © Lanvin Estate.

'Almée': Jeanne Lanvin designed this outfit for the actress Cécile Sorel to take with her on tour to Egypt. It consists of a silk coat edged with fur over a gold lace and pink crepe-de-chine dress. A sash is held in place on the hips with a large jeweled clasp, and finished with a fringe of pearls. Gouache. © Lanvin Estate.

A long cape made in 1937, showing the couture house's continuing attachment to the embroidery and beadwork with which it made its name. *Vogue* 1937. © Lanvin Estate.

After converting Jeanne Lanvin's mansion in Rue Barbet-de-Jouy, Armand-Albert Rateau collaborated with her on the design of the Lanvin Décoration shop at 15 Rue du Faubourg Saint-Honoré. This **carved wooden panel** was part of the gilded lift cage. © Lanvin Estate.

Carved oak panel with a *garçonne*, part of the decoration of the entrance to the Lanvin Décoration shop, made in the Armand-Albert Rateau workshops. © Lanvin Estate.

Detail of a silk taffeta dress, Winter 1922. Jeanne Lanvin's embroidered designs echo personal memories: a journey, a visit to a museum, the study of a plant form, and so on. © The Victoria and Albert Museum.

An embroidered red velvet coat, edged with fur, made for Cécile Sorel for her Egyptian tour. Gouache. © Lanvin Estate.

Jeanne Lanvin's office, photographed in 1946 by Roger Schall. This was the heart of the couture house, furnished by the famous Eugène Printz. Lanvin thought out her ideas here and made her preliminary sketches. The shelves are filled with all kinds of records, books, embroideries, clothes and lengths of cloth gathered from all over the world. © Photo Roger Schall. **The hands of Jeanne Lanvin**, photographed in her seventieth year by Kollar. 'She has extraordinary hands, the most beautiful I have ever seen; the tips of her fingers turn up towards the sky,' said Yvonne Printemps, one of Jeanne Lanvin's clients. Photo François Kollar. © Ministère de la Culture, France. January 1997.

A collection of outfits: This gouache shows the main trends of the house in the 1920s: black and white suits, with occasional touches of the special Lanvin blue, luxurious evening coats, and *robes de style* like the one shown on the easel. © Lanvin Estate.

Evening pyjama suit: in the 1920s pyjama suits challenged the pre-eminence of gowns for evening wear. This one was made for the winter collection of 1925, in pink pongee silk with gold borders. © UFAC.

Cocktail dress of about 1924: ivory hammered silk satin appliqués. Gift of Mrs Carter Marshall Braxton, 1980. © The Metropolitan Museum of Art.
A totally refined yet opulent colour scheme of gold on white creates a subtle garment with virginal overtones. Evening gown, silk chiffon and gilded kid leather, 1936. Given by Lady Glenconner. © The Victoria and Albert Museum.

Linen pyjama suit. Madame Robert Esnault-Pelterie, one of Jeanne Lanvin's clients, photographed in 1933 by Hoyningen-Huene. The red linen trousers and contrasting top are strikingly modern. Lanvin Estate. © Hamilton Photographers Ltd.
A black hat. Because of her beginnings in millinery, Jeanne Lanvin never lost her interest in hats; her couture house continued to make them. The originality of this 1923 style lies in the clever folding of the material. Gouache. © Lanvin Estate.

Sphinx: from the 1930s onwards Jeanne Lanvin's designs had a more and more pared-down quality, dramatized by clever contrasts of colour and materials. This sphinx-like headdress attracted a lot of attention in the 1936 Winter Collection; it was made of silver lamé sewn on to black tulle, turning into a cape collar on the long black crepe dress. *Vogue* 1936. © Lanvin Estate.
'Les Allées', a sports outfit: in response to the gradual emancipation of women, Jeanne Lanvin made some clothes suitable for new activities, like this sports blouse of 1930. © Lanvin Estate.

The success of 'Arpège' encouraged Jeanne Lanvin to develop her perfume business, and she was quick to start using **photographs for her publicity**. This one by Meerson shows the consistency of style linking the perfumes and the clothes. The gadroon motif is seen on the stoppers of the bottles and on the sleeves of the dress. Photo by Meerson. © Lanvin Estate. **Satin evening jacket with top stitching**. During the 1930s Jeanne Lanvin made increasing use of top-stitching effects. The decoration on the button recalls the stopper of the 'Arpège' bottle. Gift of Mrs John Guinness. © The Victoria and Albert Museum.

The bedroom and boudoir of Jeanne Lanvin's mansion. All the rooms were designed by Armand-Albert Rateau with great aesthetic freedom and concern for comfort. The walls were covered with 'Lanvin-blue' shantung silk embroidered with palmettes and daisies in white and silver silk thread; paintings by famous artists and personal photographs hung side by side. This room setting was given to the Musée des Arts Decoratifs in 1965 by Louis de Polignac. The museum, with the help of the house of Lanvin, has guaranteed its preservation. © Lanvin Estate. **Winter 1934 outfits**. © Photo Lipnitzki-Viollet.

A gold lamé dress made for the Bal de la Parure of 1925; its decorations of velvet and silk flowers underline the delicate femininity of the style. © Photo Sarah Moon.
Evening dress, about 1930. Light green taffeta and silk net. Gift of Mrs Jill L. Leinbach and James L. Long in memory of their mother, Mrs Jane P. Long, 1986. © The Metropolitan Museum of Art.

Detail of the sleeve. © Photo Laziz Hamani. This startlingly modern dress called **'My Fair Lady'**, was shown at the 1939 Exhibition in San Francisco. White organdie bias-cut ribbon was sewn on to a black background, giving the effect of a series of folds. It had a large black taffeta bow at the back. Lanvin Estate. © Photo Laziz Hamani.

This **tea-gown** of 1929 is a foretaste of Jeanne Lanvin's work in the 1930s, with its simple lines, attention to detail in the use of fabrics, and the emergence of lamé. The outfit consists of a pleated underskirt of pink georgette, a long tunic in silver lamé, with a jacket of silver piqué georgette. Photo Hoyningen-Huene. © Hamilton Photographers Ltd.
'La Nuit de Paris', 1926. A design worn by Jeanne Renouard, director of the Théâtre Daunou; the original interior of the theatre, designed by Jeanne Lanvin and Armand-Albert Rateau in 1921, has been preserved. © Lanvin Estate.

This **outfit of pale pink georgette**, decorated with diamond shapes of silver and diamanté beading, was worn by Valentine Tessier in the role of Alcmène in Jean Giradoux's play *Amphitryon 38*. Lanvin Estate. © Photo Laziz Hamani. The extreme simplicity of the shape of this **silver lamé hat** is underlined by its minutely worked beading. It dates from the 1920s, when there was a vogue for an 'Italian Renaissance' style. Lanvin Estate. © Photo Laziz Hamani.

Jeanne Lanvin made a number of adaptable garments to be worn according to the mood of her clients, such as this **short jacket with a detachable cape** made of leopard skin in 1935. Gouache. © Lanvin Estate.
The beautiful **Lee Miller in a Lanvin evening dress**, at the time of her liaison with the photographer Man Ray. Photograph by Hoyningen-Huene for *Vogue*, 1932. © Hamilton Photographers Ltd.

A 1938 **advertisement for Lanvin Tailleur**, in the magazine *Plaisirs de France*. It shows an elegant gentleman choosing from the range of clothing available from the men's department since 1926. © Lanvin Estate.
Marie-Blanche and the comte Jean de Polignac. Marguerite, renamed Marie-Blanche, married the comte de Polignac in 1925. They were the centre of a large group of celebrities and artists. © Photo Roger Schall. Archives Lanvin.

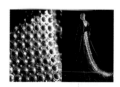

Gown detail, 1937: The inspiration for this sequin design probably came from one of the many traditional costumes that Jeanne Lanvin had collected. © Photo Laziz Hamani. At the 1937 Exposition Universelle, Jeanne Lanvin supervised the section covering couture, furs, perfumery and men's fashion. She showed this impressive **gown of black taffeta**; its wide kimono sleeves and the long sequined band running from the nape of the neck to the very end of the train gave it a regal air. © Photo Laziz Hamani.

The books filled with carefully collected records of all the beading, embroideries and gouache sketches, date from the foundation of the couture house in 1909; they constitute the Lanvin memoir, and represent an inexhaustible resource for research and inspiration. Lanvin Estate. © Photo Laziz Hamani.
Geometric design on coral and orange embroidery on black taffeta, from 1921. This motif was utilized often in the twenties, using white beads, mother of pearl or turquoise. Lanvin Estate. © Photo Laziz Hamani.

The publishers would like
to thank the House of Lanvin
for its help in the preparation
of this book, and particularly
Gérald Asaria, Odile Fraigneau
and Rosine.

Thanks are also due to Laziz
Hamani, Sarah Moon and Roger
Schall (Studio Schall).

Finally, this book would not
have been possible without the
help and efficiency of Madame
Lajournade (Roger-Viollet),
Marie-Hélène Poix (UFAC),
Joanne Noon and Tatiana Robbin
(Hamilton Photographers
Limited) and Michèle Zaquin
(*Vogue* France).